Manual
of
Field Education

Attention Authors

Our message to the world is that India can win the battle not only by the bullet but also by the pen. There is no dearth of intellectuals in our country, but their knowledge is confined to them only. No sincere effort has been made by any other publisher to channelise their knowledge in national interest. That is why the talent of a large number of intellectuals remains latent. An author transforms his knowledge into a manuscript, and it is our job to spread his/her knowledge by converting it into a beautiful book. We are constantly motivating the intellectuals for writing/ publishing their manuscripts and would like to publish your manuscript too. If you or your colleagues have any manuscript ready for publication or are working on it, kindly contact us with detailed synopsis and list of contents. We will transform your work into a valuable publication. If you wish, we can also suggest you the suitable subjects for writing the books related to your area of expertise. We are known for publishing quality and commitments. We take utmost care in production and give wide publicity to the book as well as its author through our national and international distribution network.

Manual of Field Education

Tracy Clark

Books for Libraries
Delhi-110042

Books for Libraries

B-221, Shahbad Daulatpur,
Near Vikram Dharam Kanta
Delhi-110042
Ph: 9868224781
E-mail: booksforlibraries@hotmail.com

Tracy Clark

2014

ISBN : 978-81-926482-3-1

₹ 495/-

Printed in India at
HS Offsets, Delhi
and published by Mrs Rekha Garg for
Books For Libraries, B-221, Shahbad Daulatpur,
Near Vikram Dharam Kanta,
New Delhi-110042 (INDIA)

Contents

Preface

Dear Social Work Students, Field Instructors, and Field Liaisons: Welcome to the Field Education Manual of the School of Social Work at Minnesota State University Moorhead. The field education process involves the active collaboration of three parties, the students preparing for and doing internship or field experience, the field instructors who are teaching and supervising these students, and the field liaisons from the social work department who monitor the students' progress during placement, with the common goal of a positive and educational experience for everyone involved. Field education is different from other university courses our students experience, as the instruction is primarily learning by doing. Students finally have a chance to apply their book knowledge to actual practice in the field, developing their social work skills and values in the process.

The undergraduate Social Work program at MSUM has been accredited by the Council on Social Work Education since 1973. The purpose of our program is to offer students a high quality education that teaches social work knowledge, skills, and values requisite for entry-level generalist social work practice. The Social Work faculty is committed to baccalaureate social work education, and recognizes the field experience as an integral part of that education. Equally committed to the field education program are the field instructors, who work directly with our students in the field placements. Without their time, effort and expertise, our students would not receive that crucial part of their social work education. Thank you, field instructors, for your personal and professional contribution to the Social Work program at MSUM. This manual is designed to provide students, field instructors and liaisons all the information that is needed for the internship and field experience. All forms used in field education are in the back of the manual and can be downloaded. Hopefully this manual will assist you and give clarification to your roles and responsibilities to facilitate a successful outcome. The Social Work faculty at MSUM wishes all of you a very rewarding field education experience.

Tracy Clark

Chapter 1

Introductory Information on the Social Work Program

A. **Mission and Program Competencies**
B. **School of Social Work**
C. **Social Work Curriculum**
D. **Students Rights**
E. **Student Responsibilities**

A. Mission and Program Competencies

Mission Statement

The Minnesota State University Moorhead (MSUM) Social Work program prepares competent and effective professionals for entry-level generalist social work practice, and provides leadership in developing service delivery systems and advancing social and economic justice.

Program Core Competencies

The MSUM School of Social Work's curricular design is a competency-based outcome performance approach designed to integrate and apply measurable practice behaviors with the goal of preparing its graduates for BSW generalist practice through demonstration of the achievement of the following core competencies:

MSUM baccalaureate social work program graduates will be able to:

1. Identify as a professional social worker and conduct oneself accordingly;
2. Apply social work ethical principles to guide professional practice;
3. Apply critical thinking to inform and communicate professional judgments;
4. Engage diversity and difference in practice;
5. Advance human rights and social and economic justice;
6. Engage in research-informed practice and practice informed research;
7. Apply knowledge of human behavior and the social environment;
8. Engage in policy practice to advance social and economic well-being and to deliver effective social work services;
9. Respond to contexts that shape practice;
10. Engage, assess, intervene, and evaluate with individuals, families, groups, organizations and communities;

MSUM baccalaureate School of Social Work faculty will:

11. Provide continuing education to area practitioners in order to maintain collaborative relationships with and promote continual professional development among social work practitioners, groups, organizations, communities, and practitioners of other disciplines;

12. Serve as consultants and agency board members in order to influence the delivery of social services and work to oppose oppression and discrimination, and promote social and economic justice within the university and larger community.

B. Social Work Department

Presently the School of Social Work is comprised of four full time faculty and approximately 250 undergraduate majors. One full-time office manager, a part-time faculty assistant, and several work-study students provide invaluable support to faculty and students. The School of Social Work offers a Title IV- E Child Welfare stipend which supports students who want to pursue a career in child welfare services. The School also sponsors two active student social work organizations: Dragon SOS (Dragon Society of Social Workers) and Phi Alpha.

We invite you to find out more about our department by visiting our web site at www.mnstate.edu/socialwork.

C. MSUM Social Work Curriculum

Each student entering Internship will have taken the following core social work courses. Many students will have also had various social work elective courses. A grade of C- or better must be attained in these courses.

Social Work 250 - Introduction to Social Welfare

This course provides an overview of the social welfare system, the profession, and the practice of social work. The generalist practice problem-solving model used throughout the curriculum is introduced.

Social Work 330 - Human Behavior and the Social Environment

This course enables students to integrate social,

behavioral, and human biological knowledge in the assessment of people interacting with their environment.

Social Work Department Admission

Admission to the department occurs after the student has taken SW 250 and is taking SW 330. In addition, the student has completed a variety of prerequisite courses, has a 2.5 or better GPA, has demonstrated basic writing skills, and has completed a minimum of 30 hours human service experience. Students must gain admission to the department before they are allowed to take further core social work courses.

Social Work 400 Research Methods in Social Work

This course provides social work students with an understanding of research methods and processes, which can be applied to their social work practice.

Social Work 420 Generalist Practice with Individuals

This course focuses on teaching basic interviewing skills including communication and relationship skills that are necessary in using the generalist practice model with individuals in practice. Audiotape and videotape exercises are used to enhance learning.

Social Work 430 Generalist Practice with Families

This course is designed to give students beginning competency in using the generalist practice problem-solving model with the family as the client. Students learn various family assessment tools. Students also explore their own families of origin to become aware of how issues from those systems might influence their social work practice.

Social Work 440 Generalist Practice with Groups

This course introduces students to social group work.

Content includes an introduction to group theory and dynamics, group roles, group interventions, the various types of social work with groups and group work skills. Students participate in an on-going interactional group to practice leadership and membership skills.

Social Work 450 Generalist Practice with Communities and Organizations

This course is designed to develop beginning skills for working with larger systems. Students work in planning groups to develop a formalized project proposal in which a social problem is identified, analyzed and a change effort is planned.

Social Work 460 Social Welfare Policy

This course provides knowledge of selected policy areas and knowledge of the process by which policy is formed. This class contributes to students making informed and professionally ethical policy decisions in the provision of services and participation in change.

Social Work 469 Internship

After students have completed the core social work courses and electives and have attained a grade of C- or better in these courses and all related requirements, 90 hours of human service experience, and maintain a 2.5 or better GPA, they can apply for internship.

There are three mandatory meetings held the semester prior to internship which assist the student in preparing for, finding, and confirming an internship for the following semester. Internship requires a minimum of 480 hours at an agency under the supervision of a social worker.

Social Work 470 Senior Seminar

This seminar is taken concurrently with internship and

focuses on ethical social work practice. It also provides students the opportunity to discuss the practical, personal and professional concerns of their internship experiences.

D. Student Rights

MSUM Student Handbook 2010/2011

Members of the University community are expected to be familiar with the rules and procedures contained within this handbook. This publication provides general guidance and direction, and it is not intended to cover every conceivable situation. The information about University policies outlines the rights, responsibilities, and privileges enjoyed by the students, faculty, and staff that make up the University community. The purpose of MSUM's policies is to promote and maintain the University learning environment, inform University members of their responsibilities, and aid in preventing violations of the rights of individuals.

Specific questions relating to policies, procedures, and interpretations of specific sections within the Handbook should be directed to the University Judicial Affairs Officer at (218) 477-2174 or the Vice President for Student Affairs at (218) 477-2171.

Because policies are subject to change, revisions that occur will be updated on the MSUM webpage and will have priority over the contents of the printed edition.

Minnesota State University Moorhead believes students have certain rights. These rights are as follows:

1. Freedom to Learn

In addition to the basic constitutional rights enjoyed by all citizens, students in colleges and universities have specific rights related to academic freedom and their status as students. Freedom to teach and freedom to learn are inseparable facets of academic freedom. The freedom to learn depends upon appropriate opportunities and conditions in the classroom, on the campus, and in the larger community. Students are expected to exercise their freedom with responsibility.

2. Freedom of Expression

Individual students and student organizations shall be free to examine and to discuss all questions of interest to them and to express opinions publicly and privately. They shall be free to support causes by orderly means that do not substantially disrupt the regular and essential operation of the institution. Students shall be free to take reasoned exception to the data or views offered in any course of study and to reserve judgment about matters of opinion, but they are responsible for learning the content of any course of study for which they are enrolled.

3. Freedom of Association

Students shall be free to organize and join organizations to promote their common and lawful interests, subject to institutional policies or regulations. Registration or recognition may be withheld or withdrawn from organizations that violate institutional regulations.

4. Student-Sponsored Forums

Students shall have the right to assemble, to select speakers, and to discuss issues of their choice. The college or university shall establish reasonable time, place and manner restrictions to assure that the assembly does not substantially disrupt the work of the institution or does not interfere with the opportunity of other students to obtain an education or otherwise infringe upon the rights of others. Such regulations shall not be used as a means of censorship.

The president or designee may prohibit any forum when there is a likelihood of harm to individuals or damage to property if the event is held. Prior to any such prohibition, the president shall make his or her best effort to consult with the student association.

5. Student Publications

Student-funded publications shall be free of censorship and advance approval of copy, and their editors and managers shall be free to develop their own editorial and news coverage policies. Editors and managers of student publications shall be protected from arbitrary suspension and removal because of student, faculty, administrative, or public disapproval of editorial policy or content.

The student fee allocation process shall not be used as a means of editorial control of student-funded publications. All student publications shall explicitly state on the editorial page that the opinions there expressed are not necessarily those of the college, university, system, or student body.

6. Student Policies

The policies of the college or university regarding student expectations, rights and responsibilities shall be readily accessible to students.

7. Catalog and Course Information

To the extent possible, students shall be provided relevant and accurate information regarding courses prior to enrollment. Catalog descriptions and website postings shall be accurate and based on information existing at the time of publication. To the extent possible, class schedules shall list the names of faculty teaching courses.

8. Student Academic Standing Information

Students shall have access to accurate information for

establishing and maintaining acceptable academic standing, information which will enable students to determine their individual academic standing, and information regarding graduation requirements.

9. Academic Evaluation

Student academic performance shall be evaluated solely on the basis of academic standards, including any requirements that are noted in the catalog, course syllabus, or student handbook. Students shall have protection against prejudiced or capricious evaluation and shall not be evaluated on the basis of opinions or conduct in matters unrelated to academic standards.

Students shall have the right to review their corrected examinations or other required assignments used by the faculty in evaluating the student's academic performance.

10. Property Rights

Term papers, essays, projects, works of art, and similar property including property in which the student has intellectual property rights pursuant to Board Policy 3.26 shall be returned to a student upon request, within a reasonable timeframe, when no longer needed for evaluation purposes, unless the student grants written permission for them to be retained.

11. Student Review and Consultation

Students shall have the right to appropriate levels of participation in college and university decision-making pursuant to Policy 2.3 and Procedure 2.3.1, Student Involvement in Decision-Making. (Minnesota State Colleges and Universities: Board Policies; Chapter 3 – Educational Policies)

E. Student Responsibilities

MSUM Student Handbook 2010/2011

Minnesota State University Moorhead supports the concept of educational discipline. The University has a duty to protect its educational purpose by setting standards of scholarship and conduct. The guiding principle of University regulations is to promote student responsibility and accountability.

The University views the student conduct process as a learning experience that promotes growth and personal understanding of one's responsibilities and privileges within the University community. Therefore, it is the responsibility of the student who has been accused of misconduct to participate conscientiously in the discipline process. Students are responsible for becoming familiar with University policies and procedures. Failure to be informed does not excuse misconduct.

MSUM standards of conduct are published here as the Code of Conduct. In all conduct proceedings it is recognized that MSUM is an educational institution and not a court of law. This code does not replace or reduce the requirements of civil or criminal laws. All criminal activity may be referred to local law enforcement as well as investigated internally. Members of the University community also have responsibilities as citizens. Violations that constitute crimes and the annual crime report can be found at: http://www.mnstate.edu/security/annualcrime.cfm

* Being under the influence of alcohol and/or other drugs does not in any way excuse or mitigate responsibility for a student's behavior. The excessive, illegal, unprescribed or otherwise socially irresponsible use of alcohol or other drugs infringes upon one's ability to preserve personal integrity and civility.

* Disciplinary action is cumulative resulting in more serious consequences if the student engages in repeat violations or fails to follow through with sanctions from a previous hearing.

Minnesota State University Moorhead's non-academic university performance standards and the School of Social Work's non-academic performance standards are also outlined in the *Social Work Student Handbook.* All students are held equally to the academic and non-academic performance standards and each student's continuance in the Social Work program is determined by her or his suitability for professional social work practice as judged by social work faculty, and as evidenced by acceptable performance while in the program. *(Social Work Student Handbook)*

Social work students are also responsible for adhering to the standards of the NASW Code of Ethics. This Code is made available to the students in the Admissions packet, and is discussed in detail in SW 470 Senior Seminar.

Notes

Chapter 2

Policies and Procedures to the Field Education Program

A. University Internship Policies
B. Social Work Department Internship Requirements
C. Criteria for Selection of Agencies and Field Instructors
D. Procedure for Placing and Monitoring Students
E. Procedure for Evaluation of Student Learning in the Field
F. Procedure for non-BSW or MSW Field Instructors
G. Field Instruction Training
H. Policy Regarding Field Placement and Employment
I. Policy Regarding Long Distance Internships
J. Statement on Sexual Harassment
K. Student Liability Insurance for Internships
L. Policy Regarding Student Medical Insurance

A. University Internship Policies

MSUM Bulletin

Minnesota State University Moorhead requires that students must: be junior or senior status when taking an internship for credit, be a major in the department granting internship credit, and meet internship standards set by individual academic departments and any departmental requirements related to internship planning and follow-up.

Internship credit will be awarded on the basis of at least 40 hours of field work per semester credit. The maximum number of credits allowed for internship is 12 semester credits. Please see the MSUM Bulletin for more detailed information about Internship.

B. School of Social Work Internship Requirements

To register for internship, students must have successfully completed all required course work and obtain a C- of better in social work courses, 90 hours of human service requirement, and have an overall MSUM GPA of 2.5 or better. While internship is a required capstone experience that all students must successfully complete to receive their BSW degree, it must also be highlighted that it is a privilege to engage in this learning experience and not an absolute right.

Therefore, students will be evaluated on all academic and non-academic standards (as defined in sections N and O of the policies and procedures) both prior to and during their internship placement. Internship privileges can and may be reevaluated or revoked if it is deemed appropriate and/or necessary under our existing policy guidelines. Internship is a block placement usually occurring in the student's last academic semester. It requires a minimum of 464 hours at a human services setting/agency under the supervision of a social worker. In the case that the field instructor is not a social worker but has a degree in a related discipline, special consideration is given to enable the student to do the internship. Field Practicum courses may not be transferred from an unaccredited to an accredited program.

C. Criteria for Selection of Agencies and Field Instructors

Internship must occur in settings that reinforce students' identification with the purposes, values, and ethics of the profession, foster the integration of empirical and practice-based knowledge, and promote the development of professional competence.

The School of Social Work requires that all agencies used for field education provide a sanctioned social service or criminal justice program. These agencies are required to provide qualified personnel to be assigned as "Field Instructors" for the student interns.

Primary, as well as secondary, social work settings are utilized for the internship program. The most frequently used agencies include the area county social services, area schools, hospitals, and nursing homes, and many of the non-profit agencies such as Lutheran Social Services, Lakeland Mental Health, Head-Start, PATH, as well as many others.

The School of Social Work requires that field instructors have a college degree, preferably a Bachelor's or Master's degree in Social Work. If the field instructor does not possess a social work degree, he/she agrees to provide a field experience that is consistent with social work values and ethics. Students who have field instructors who do not have a BSW or MSW are required to meet with their field liaisons on a monthly basis during internship for additional supervision and instruction.

In addition, if a student is awarded a Child Welfare Stipend through the School of Social Work, they are held responsible, in coordination with the Child Welfare Coordinator, for meeting the following additional requirements prior to and during internship:

- have a senior field practicum in a county or stated child welfare unit;
- complete a child welfare course;
- attend child welfare IV-E student meetings and seminars if applicable;
- maintain good academic standing (as defined by the social work departmental policy); and
- upon exit from the social work department seek and accept employment in public child welfare (if such a position is available and offered within three months of graduation and maintain such employment for four and a half months for each semester that they received a stipend)

D. Procedure for Placing and Monitoring Students

Preparation for internship occurs in three meetings involving the field coordinator and prospective interns one semester prior to internship. These meetings are required for all students planning to do their internship the following semester.

The procedure for placement is student directed; the students choose their own placements within certain parameters. They are allowed significant latitude in choosing a site that will best meet their personal learning objectives. However, before an internship is finalized the student meets with the field coordinator to confirm that the agency meets with department approval.

Students research the types of internship placement that interest them. They may choose, but are not limited to child welfare agencies, family service agencies, mental health programs, criminal justice settings, programs serving elderly persons, programs serving developmentally disabled persons, medical social work, school social work, drug and alcohol treatment programs, institutional treatment settings, and community organizing.

Once an internship placement is agreed upon, a contract is formalized which clarifies the expectations of the student, the agency, and the School of Social Work. This contract is signed by all three parties and kept in the student's internship file.

Social work student interns are monitored by field liaisons who conduct two formal site visits during the semester. The field liaison is also available for phone contacts and additional visits if the need arises. Field Liaisons will meet with interns whose field instructors are not BSW or MSW degreed, on a monthly basis to provide additional supervision and instruction from the social work perspective. These meetings can occur on Fridays following Senior Seminar class, or at other arranged times.

Field liaisons are full time faculty from the social work department.

E. Procedure for Evaluation of Student Learning in the Field

Students are placed in agencies under the supervision of experienced social services professionals. This allows students to obtain on-going feedback and formal evaluation of their social work knowledge and practice behaviors.

The student intern will be formally evaluated twice during the semester, at midterm and the end of the semester. Evaluation of the internship experience reflects the students' ability to achieve successful integration and application of the ten program competencies (see page 34 for a detailed listing) in an actual practice setting. Each program competency will ultimately be evaluated by rating the related practice behaviors associated with it (see page 35 for a detailed listing of the practice behaviors).

These evaluations use a Likert scale to rate each specific social work practice behaviors. This evaluation format will provide students feedback on how they are performing in selected areas, and assist them in identifying those areas that need further development. The Internship Workbook is designed to help guide both the field instructor and the student in their formal evaluation of the 41 practice behaviors. In addition, each goal has space for any narrative comments the field instructor may have pertaining to the goal.

The field instructor, upon completing the written evaluation, will meet with the stu ent to discuss the evaluation and answer any question the student may have. Students will also rate themselves using this same form. At the evaluation meeting, the field instructor and the student can then compare their ratings and utilize the discussion for further learning. The student should remember that the evaluations are not grades.

This is an opportunity for feedback and for students to learn a great deal about themselves as potential social workers. Students are strongly encouraged to take maximal advantage of this opportunity. Although the internship evaluations are not grades, the interns' Pass/Fail status will be partially determined by the formal final evaluation results.

Field Instructor Evaluation

The student intern will provide the field instructor with two formal evaluation forms. The midterm evaluation will occur during the eighth week of the semester and the final evaluation will occur the last week of the semester.

Students will be evaluated on the ten program competencies through their successful achievement of the 41 practice behaviors of internship. Field Instructors are required to meet and discuss with the student both the mid-term and final evaluations. Upon review and discussion of the evaluation, both parties must sign the Field Instructor Evaluation form.

The Internship Workbook is designed to help guide both the field instructor and the student in their formal evaluation of the 41 practice behaviors. The evaluation forms can be found in section VII of the Field Manual. The student is responsible for getting this form to the field instructor on a timely basis. The student is also responsible to ensure that these written evaluations reach the field liaison at midterm and the final week of internship.

Student Self Evaluation

Each student will complete two self-evaluations, once at midterm and again at the end of internship. This is the student's assessment of her/his personal learning during the internship in regards to meeting the ten program competencies. The field instructor and student intern will use the same evaluation form in section VII. As stated in the Field Instructor Evaluation section, they will meet and discuss the evaluations with their Field Instructor and both parties must sign the Student Evaluation form. The student will turn all evaluations into the field liaison at the appropriate designated time of the semester. The field instructor's evaluation, both midterm and final, become part of the student's permanent file.

F. Procedure for non-BSW or MSW Field Instructors

Field instructors who do not hold a MSW or BSW degree but have a college degree in a related field such as human services, criminal justice, counseling, or psychology, agree to provide a field experience which is consistent with social work values and ethics.

These field instructors are required to attend the Field Instructor Orientation meeting and to work closely with the field liaison in order to provide an internship experience that identifies with the purposes, values, and ethics of the social work profession.

Students who have non-MSW or BSW field instructors are invited and encouraged to meet once a month with their field liaisons in addition to the two site visits to assure that the student is getting sufficient social work supervision.

In addition, the non-MSW or BSW field instructors are given a packet of materials put together by the field coordinator. This packet includes an information sheet Social Work at Minnesota State University Moorhead, the major in Social Work – BSW Degree requirements, the NASW Code of Ethics, and excerpts from Bogo and Vayda's book, The Practice of Field Instruction in Social Work, and Kirst-Ashman and Hull's *Understanding General Practice.*

G. Field Instruction Training

Field instructors are invited to participate in training seminars and workshops designed by the School of Social Work. These seminars are held every spring semester. Flyers or invitations to these seminars go out to all field instructors. The field coordinator, with the assistance of the Social Work faculty, offers a variety of topics at these annual seminars. Topics of previous seminars have been: Making the Connection : Linking Theory and Practice, Ethics, and Racial Identity Development. These seminars last for two to three hours, and certificates of attendance are made available to attendees.

The field coordinator offers the field instructor orientation seminar every academic semester. The agenda at these meetings include: information about the internship; clarification of the roles of the field instructor, the field liaison, and the field coordinator; review of the syllabus, goals, written assignments, and evaluations for internship; review of the policies for termination of an internship, sexual harassment, and internship liability insurance. The orientation lasts about an hour and a half. New field instructors are required to attend this orientation seminar, and all field instructors are encouraged to attend.

H. Policy Regarding Field Placement and Employment

Student assignments and field education supervision must differ from those associated with the student's employment. For this reason, any placement that occurs at an agency where the student is also employed, it is required that the student does not use their employment as their internship. It is further required that the student be involved in a different program and have a different supervisor than their employment. Field placements in agencies where students are also employed are monitored closely by the field coordinator and the student's field liaison.

However, if a student becomes hired during the internship in the area that internship is occurring, he/she may continue in the internship setting in a paid position as long as the terms of the internship are carried out, assignments are turned in, and the evaluations are completed as scheduled by the field instructor and the student.

I. Policy Regarding Long Distance Internships

Students are not allowed to do their internships beyond a radius of 250 miles from MSUM, thus giving our program opportunity to adequately monitor the placement and the student. Some students take Senior Seminar, a three-credit course that runs concurrently with internship, at accredited schools of social work other than MSUM and closer to their internship. For example, students doing internship in St. Cloud or Minneapolis may register and take Senior Seminar at St. Cloud University.

It is the student intern's responsibility to initiate the enrollment process with another university and social work program. However, all students register for SW 469: Internship through MSUM and are followed by field liaisons from the MSUM School of Social Work. Students taking SW 470 Senior Seminar at another institution must follow these guidelines:

a. it must be a CSWE accredited school of social work;

b. it must be equivalent to three semester course credits; and

c. it should have a practice evaluation component

J. Statement on Sexual Harassment

"Acts of sexual discrimination/harassment and/or violence create an environment contrary to the goals and mission of the University. Minnesota State University

Moorhead will not tolerate such acts. These acts may also constitute criminal behavior that can be prosecuted under Minnesota law, as well as form the basis for discipline or other corrective action under employee disciplinary standards or the University student conduct code." (MSUM Affirmative Action Office 2008).

The Social Work Department expects the placement agency to follow the university's policy with regard to harassment, violence and intolerance. This expectation is made clear at the Field Instructor's Orientation meeting as well as in this manual.

K. Student Liability Insurance for Internship

Students are covered under the University's student liability insurance:

> "Students are clearly liable for their actions and may be sued (along with others) for damages due to negligence. Minnesota State University Moorhead has a Student Professional Liability Policy which covers students engaged in internships. The coverage is for $1,000,000 per occurrence and $3,000,000 in aggregate. If the student or his/her academic department or clinical practicum site does not have a formal internship agreement, and therefore does not have a formally acknowledged internship (i.e. no credit hours, etc.), the student is NOT covered by the University Student Professional Liability Policy. Students completing their practicum work in area schools can receive liability insurance through the Education Minnesota Student Program provided they are members. For more information, check out their Web site at www.mnstate.edu/emsp/." (Taken from the *MSUM Bulletin* 2010/2011, p. 56)

Students may join the National Association of Social Workers (NASW) and take out the professional liability insurance with the NASW Insurance Trust. This particular insurance is available only to individual students, and protects them for duties and field placements which are parts of their school curriculum. The limits of liability are $1,000,000/$1,000,000. This is NOT required.

L. Policy Regarding Student Medical Coverage

MSUM does not provide medical insurance coverage for any injuries that may occur during internship or the course of field placement unless the student intern has elected to purchase medical coverage from the University.

M. Internship Formal Agreement

"Before the starting date of the Internship, the Internship Supervisor, the Site Evaluator, and the Student Intern shall sign an Internship Agreement which outlines mutual responsibilities and expectations for the internship and contains statements clearly articulating liability assumption on the part of MSUM, the Site, and the Student Intern. (MSUM Bulletin 2010/2011)

The Internship/ Field Experience Contract with Placement Agencies form which appears in Section VII of this manual, clearly delineates the agreement made with the student, the agency, and the university, to include expectations from all three parties. The contract is signed by all three parties and the original copy is kept in the student's internship file. No student is allowed to begin his/ her internship without a completed contract in place.

N. The Formative Performance Evaluation Process

The Social Work Department utilizes a formative, or

process evaluation model, rather than a summative model. The intent of the faculty is to assess students' performance throughout the curriculum, and to move students toward successful completion of the program, or toward the selection of another major. Academic assessment is done in each social work course by the assignment of a grade, ranging from A+ to F, with the exception of internship which is graded either pass or fail. In addition to an ongoing academic assessment, students are formatively assessed non-academically both in and outside of the classroom. The following performance standards are used when considering each student's suitability for professional social work, and continuation in the social work program.

1. MSUM's non-academic university performance standards:

    1. Academic Integrity
    2. Computer Misuse
    3. Complicity in Prohibited acts
    4. Disruption of Operations of the University
    5. Disruptive Behavior
    6. Disruptive Demonstration
    7. Drug Paraphernalia
    8. Distribution of Illegal Drugs
    9. False Complaint
    10. Falsification of Records/Representation
    11. Fire/Arson
    12. Gambling
    13. Hazing
    14. Interfering with Judicial Procedures
    15. Laws and Ordinances

16. Official Compliance
17. Physical Harm and Threat
18. Harassment and Sexual Harassment
19. Sexual Violence
20. Skateboarding, In-line skates, and Bicycles
21. Stalking
22. Theft, Vandalism, Defacement and Damage to Property
23. Unauthorized Use of University Property
24. Psychological/Emotional Abuse
25. Unlawful Use and Possession of Alcohol
26. Unlawful Use and Possession of Drugs
27. Unlawful Use or Possession of weapons/firearms

2. Social Work Program's non-academic performance standards:

a. Breach of NASW Code of Ethics
b. Clear violation of client confidentiality
c. Current chemical abuse
d. Conditions (i.e., mental health problems. that interfere with student functioning
e. Sexual involvement with a client
f. Failure to respect interpersonal boundaries with others (i.e., students, faculty, placement staff, clients, etc.)
g. Inability to master the skills necessary for acceptable social work practice
h. Inability to relate to faculty
i. Inability to relate to clientele
j. Inability to relate to other students

In the case of a deficiency during internship, a formative evaluation process may be used before termination of the internship is decided, if the following conditions are present:

1. The deficiency is such that remediation can occur. This decision will be made jointly by the field instructor and the field liaison.
2. The field instructor is willing to work with the student in the remediation plan.

If the above conditions prevail, the course of action is as follows:

1. A meeting will be held with the student, the student's advisor, the field coordinator and/or field liaison, and if appropriate, the student's field instructor. The deficiency will be addressed and a formal notice given to the student. The remediation plan will be discussed at this meeting as well as a prescribed time frame, to be agreed upon by the student, the field coordinator, and the student's advisor.
2. In the event that the process of the remediation is not followed by the student, the field coordinator may recommend termination of the internship.
3. In the event that the concerns are so serious that they are brought to the attention of the entire faculty, the faculty may recommend termination of the student from the program.
4. The Social Work Department utilizes the university appeals policy and students involved in this process have the right to appeal any department decision.

The Formative Performance Evaluation notice and remediation plan forms can be found in the back of the *Social Work Student Handbook.* The grievance process can also be found in the *Social Work Student Handbook.*

O. Termination of Internship / Field Experience

Most students will have little or no difficulty in following the expectations for internship. However, occasionally situations arise which are serious enough to necessitate removal of a student from field placement without using the Formative Performance Evaluation Process. The following are some (but possibly not all) of the major reasons for such removal:

1. Clear violation of client confidentiality. This does not include the sharing of information necessary for case management or knowledge integration.
2. Chemical abuse or any other condition which interferes with responsibilities to clients, the placement agency, or academic course requirements.
3. Sexual involvement with a client.
4. Repeated failure to respect interpersonal boundaries with clients or placement agency staff.
5. Chronic failure to meet the expectations of internship or field experience.
6. A determination by the field instructor, the field liaison, or the field coordinator that the student does not possess the basic skills necessary for social work practice.

A student may also be removed due to situations that are beyond his/her control, such an incapacitation due to illness or accident, or agency problems which compromise the integrity of the placement experience.

The decision to remove a student will be made by the field coordinator in consultation with the social work department chair, the field liaison, the field instructor, the student's advisor, and the student. Once the decision to remove a student has been made, the student will discontinue his/her duties at the placement agency immediately.

The student who feels he/she has been removed unjustly may appeal the decision to the social work department chair. If he/she is not satisfied with the chair's decision, the decision may be appealed to the Dean.

P. Policy on Social Work Credit for Life / Work Experiences

There is no social work credit given to students for any life/work experiences. Students are required to take all core social work courses including 12 credits of internship, regardless of their experience in the field.

Q. Background Checks

Background checks are required by Minnesota state law for students doing their internship in the state of Minnesota and an agency licensed by either the MN Department of Human Services or the MN Department of Health. Applications for these checks can be attained from the MSUM social work department at no charge to the student. Some additional agencies outside the above mentioned parameters may require background checks and these may cost the student additional fees.

Notes

Chapter 3

Preparation for Internship

A. Application for Internship

Social work students are ready to be placed in internship once they have completed the core social work courses and the related area course work (see social work curriculum, on pages 11-14) and have completed 90 hours of the Human Service Requirement. Students begin planning for internship several semesters before they enroll in the course. The Social Work Internship Priority Planning Forms are given out in SW 400: Research Methods. This completed form is reviewed and signed by the student's faculty advisor and given to the department secretary who puts the student on an internship priority list. To ensure a placement students should sign up two semesters prior to the semester they want to do an internship. If the student decides not to do an internship during the semester identified, the field coordinator should be notified as soon as possible of the desired change.

During the second week of the semester preceding internship, prospective interns will be notified of the first orientation meeting. Students are required to print the Field Manual from the School of Social Work website, fill out the internship application in Section VII, (typed or printed neatly), and bring the application with them to the orientation meeting.

To be accepted into internship, a student needs to have completed all related requirements, possess an MSUM GPA of 2.5, and have a "C-" or better in all Social Work courses and related requirements. In addition, the student must possess the basic skills and emotional maturity necessary for working with clients and staff in an internship site. If the faculty has concerns about the suitability of a prospective intern, the field coordinator will discuss these concerns with the prospective intern and develop a plan for addressing the concerns.

B. Internship Preparation Meetings

Preparation for internship occurs in three meetings involving the field coordinator and prospective interns. Students who are on the internship priority list will be notified by letter of the first meeting. These meetings are required for all students planning to do their internship the following semester. Attendance will be taken at all of the preparation meetings.

1. Orientation Meeting

This meeting will give the prospective intern an overview of the preparation and requirements for internship. The student will be expected to take much of the initiative around preparation and planning for obtaining an internship.

1. Allowing students significant latitude in choosing a site that will best meet their personal learning objectives; and
2. Simulating a job search process (students will learn about the major components involved in a social work job search).

To begin this process, students will be asked to research the types of internship placement which interest them. Students may choose, but are not limited to child welfare agencies, family service agencies, mental health programs, criminal justice settings, programs serving elderly persons, programs serving developmentally disabled persons, medical social work, school social work, drug and alcohol treatment programs, institutional treatment settings, etc. Students are encouraged to consult with the social work faculty, the field coordinator, other students and professionals from the student's human service experience sites for information on placements and opportunities.

Most students will want an internship site in the Fargo-Moorhead area, thus allowing them to take SW 470: Senior Seminar at the same time. However, students may intern as far away as 250 miles: thus allowing the field liaisons the opportunity to do site visits and monitor students progress. Students may register for or attend Senior Seminar at another CSWE accredited Social Work program. Over the years, MSUM social work students have been placed in a number of different agencies. The School of Social Work maintains files that contain information on the types of experiences an intern might gain at many different placement sites. Also, names and titles of potential field instructors, agency addresses, and agency phone numbers are maintained in these files. Students are encouraged to ask the department secretary for the location of these files.

Once students have researched their area(s) of interest, it is recommended that <u>a minimum of three potential internship sites be identified for possible interviews.</u> Although there are plenty of internship sites available in Fargo-Moorhead and the surrounding area, there may be a number of reasons why students might not obtain their first choice for an internship. Some students will obtain an internship at the first agency interviewed; others will interview four or more agencies before finding the right site.

In addition to researching potential internship sites, students will be constructing a resume which will provide information regarding their education, skills and social service experience (volunteer and paid).

This resume will be submitted to potential internship agencies prior to the internship interview. Students can utilize any resume format desired. However, if the student has never constructed a resume before, some basic rules apply.

Resume should include:

a. Relevant post high school education
b. Social work related volunteer experience
c. Paid social work related experience

Listing non-social work jobs along with dates can be useful to demonstrate reliability and industry.

The MSUM Career Services periodically sponsors resume writing workshops which many students have found quite useful. In addition, some students may wish to solicit feedback on the resume from social work faculty or a social work employer. The field coordinator will spend time in the orientation meeting reviewing several resume formats. The field coordinator will provide written comments on students' resumes.

Students are expected to turn in their resumes at the next internship preparation meeting which is the Planning Meeting.

2. Planning Meeting

One week after the orientation meeting, prospective interns will meet with the field coordinator for a planning meeting. At this meeting, the process for arranging internship will be discussed and interviewing skills will be covered.

The first step in arranging an internship will be putting together internship packets to be given to each internship site the student interviews. This packet will contain the student's resume and a letter of introduction from the field coordinator to the potential internship agency. This packet provides important information to placement agencies regarding the student's interests and prior experience.

Once the student has the information packet together, calls can be made to prospective internship sites to inquire about the possibility of an interview for internship. If the agency agrees to discuss a potential internship and an interview has been arranged, the student sends or delivers the packet to the interviewing agency 2-3 days prior to the interview.

<u>The interview is a very important piece of the internship preparation process.</u> It is a chance for the agency to learn more about the student and the student to learn more about the type of services the agency provides. Students should

plan for the interview by preparing. Students will be spending 32 hours a week for 15 weeks at their internship site. They will want to know what experiences the internship site can provide which will further their personal learning objectives. It is important to obtain some sense of the degree of compatibility or "fit" between student and agency.

Students are encouraged to choose field instructors who have a BSW or MSW. However, there are exceptions made for criminal justice, counseling, and treatment (addiction) centers, where non-social work degreed professionals serve as field instructors.

Students with non-BSW or MSW degreed field instructors will receive additional supervision from their field liaisons to insure that students maintain a social work perspective in their internship.

If the student has interviews set up with other agencies, he/she should indicate this to the agency interviewer. Some agencies will offer an internship to a student at the end of an initial interview, some will request a second interview or request some time to consider the internship placement.

If the placement is desired by a number of students, the internship agency will make a decision as to which student will be offered the internship. Regardless of the outcome, it is good professional courtesy to **thank the agency interviewer for their time and consideration,** and for answering your questions.

Once an internship has been offered to the student, she/he will arrange a short meeting with the field coordinator to discuss the placement. The student must bring information regarding the **agency name, address, phone number and name of the field instructor** on a Placement Finalization Form in section VII to the field coordinator. If the proposed placement is deemed appropriate by the field coordinator, the student will be asked to sign a Placement Agency Contract (Section VII). Formal finalization occurs between MSUM and the internship agency and is documented via the signing of the Placement Agency Contract by the field instructor, field coordinator and the student. Once a final decision regarding placement is made, the student will notify all other agencies which he/she has interviewed of his/her intent not to intern with them.

Students who arrange an internship at an agency licensed by the Minnesota Department of Human Services or the Minnesota Department of Health are required by law to complete a Minnesota Bureau of Criminal Apprehension Background Check. This Minnesota law is an effort to protect vulnerable clients from potentially abusive individuals. The student must fill out a scantron sheet and a release form to the internship agency. These two forms can be obtained from the department secretary.

3. Information Meeting

Two weeks before the end of the semester preceding internship, students will meet together with the field coordinator to discuss expectations for internship. Most of the internships should be finalized by this time, however some students may still be making internship arrangements. The internship syllabus will be reviewed in detail to ensure that the student understands the goals and expectations of internship. The assignments, the agency site visits, and the internship time line will also be discussed. Termination of internships, liability insurance, MSUM's medical insurance, and sexual harassment policy are also covered.

Any final questions that the student has about the structure, expectations, and process of internship can be addressed at this time. This is the last meeting before internship begins. Each student must, in addition to finding and finalizing their internship placement, enroll in the SW 469: Internship course. Registration codes are obtained from the student's academic advisor. Advisors will only provide registration codes to students who have submitted written verification of 90 Human Service Experience hours and can show evidence of a 2.5 MSUM GPA, with a "C-" or better in all social work courses and related requirements. Students are minimally required to be enrolled by the first day of internship.

C. Internship Preparation Flow Chart

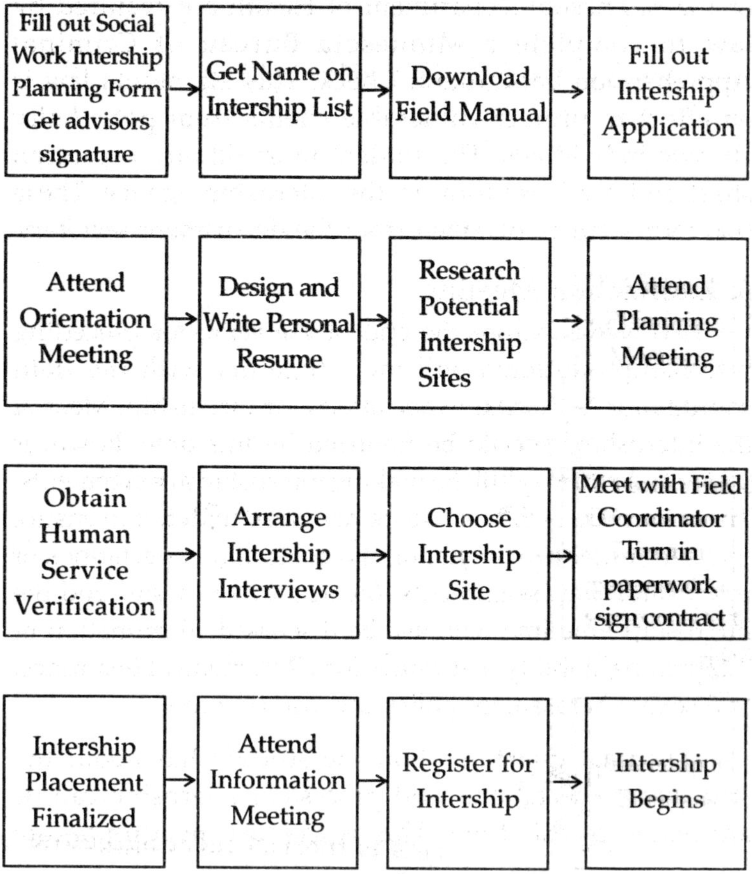

Chapter 4

Internship

A. Internship Syllabus

Minnesota State University Moorhead
Social Work Department
SW 469: Internship

Tracy Clark
Assistant Professor/ Field Coordinator
E-mail: clarkt@mnstate.edu
Office Hours: Posted on office door

Office: LI Porch
Phone: (218) 477-4002
Fax: (218) 477-2987

Mission Statement of the Social Work Department

The Minnesota State University Moorhead (MSUM) Social Work program prepares competent and effective professionals for entry-level generalist social work practice, and provides leadership in developing service delivery systems and advancing social and economic justice.

Curricular Context

The MSUM Social Work program defines generalist practice as the critical application of aneclectic knowledge base, professional values, and a wide range of culturally competent skills to a planned change process at any system level. All of the social work courses use the generalist practice intervention model as the basis for social work on all levels: individuals, families, groups, communities and organizations. SW 469 Internship occurs after all the core social work courses have been taken by students. It is a block placement where students spend 464 hours in a social work or human services setting under agency and departmental supervision. Planning for internship begins at least two semesters prior to internship.

Course Description

Internship is a 12-credit field practicum that is designed to provide social work students a practice experience in a social work or human services related agency with professional supervision. The academic supervision is provided by field liaisons from the social work faculty. Direct supervision in the field placement is provided by agency staff whom serve as field instructors for the students.

The field liaison, the field instructor and the student intern work together to design an internship experience that includes a basic introduction to social work practice and an opportunity to develop some of the student's individualized interests. This course builds on and assists in the integration of all coursework required for the social work major as well as the broader liberal arts perspective. Internship gives the students the opportunity to practice and integrate the social work knowledge, values and skills obtained in the classroom in an agency setting.

Prerequisites for internship include all the major social work course requirements to include all required prerequisites in related areas, with a "C-" or better in these courses prior to taking SW 469: Internship; completion and documentation of the 90 hours Human Service Experience requirement; an MSUM GPA of 2.5 or better; and consent.

SW 469 Internship is solidly anchored in the social work program's mission and program competencies. At the successful completion of internship, students are ready for entry-level generalist social work practice. Internship reinforces identification with social work values and ethics by holding students accountable to the NASW Code of Ethics.

Internship fosters integration of empirical and practice-based knowledge in a practice setting by giving students the opportunity to do direct micro or macro practice in an agency setting. Internship promotes development of professional competence through supervision and professional guidance of students by their field instructors.

The BSW field education/internship prepares students for generalist practice by providing competency-based education in which students will be evaluated on their achievement of the following core competencies:

Program Competencies

1. (EPAS 2.1.1). Identify as a professional social worker and conduct oneself accordingly;

2. (EPAS 2.1.2) Apply social work ethical principles to guide professional practice;
3. (EPAS 2.1.3) Apply critical thinking to inform and communicate professional judgments;
4. (EPAS 2.1.4) Engage diversity and difference in practice;
5. (EPAS 2.1.5) Advance human rights and social and economic justice;
6. (EPAS 2.1.6) Engage in research-informed practice and practice-informed research;
7. (EPAS 2.1.7) Apply knowledge of human behavior and the social environment;
8. (EPAS 2.1.8) Engage in policy practice to advance social and economic well-being and to deliver effective social work services;
9. (EPAS 2.1.9) Respond to contexts that shape practice;
10. (EPAS 2.1.10) Engage, assess, intervene, and evaluate with individuals, families, groups, organizations and communities;

Practice Behaviors

The following 41 practice behaviors provide an operationalized description of the core competencies. Each program competency will be evaluated by rating the resulting practice behaviors associated with it.

Competency 1 (EPAS 2.1.1): Identify as a professional social worker and conduct oneself accordingly.

PB 1. (2.1.1.1) Advocate for client access to the services of social work;

PB 2. (2.1.1.2) Practice personal reflection and self-correction to assure continual professional development;

PB 3. (2.1.1.3) Attend to professional roles and boundaries;

PB 4. (2.1.1.4) Demonstrate professional demeanor in behavior, appearance, and communication;

PB 5. (2.1.1.5) Engage in career-long learning;

PB 6. (2.1.1.6) Use supervision and consultation;

Competency 2 (EPAS 2.1.2): Apply social work ethical principles to guide professional practice.

PB 7. (2.1.2.1) Recognize and manage personal values in a way that allows professional values to guide practice;

PB 8. (2.1.2.2) Make ethical decisions by applying standards of NASW Code of Ethics;

PB 9. (2.1.2.3) Tolerate ambiguity in resolving ethical conflicts;

PB 10. (2.1.2.4) Apply strategies of ethical reasoning to arrive at principled decisions;

Competency 3 (EPAS 2.1.3): Apply social work ethical principles to guide professional practice.

PB 11. (2.1.3.1) Distinguish, appraise, and integrate multiple sources of knowledge, including research-based knowledge, and practice wisdom;

PB 12. (2.1.3.2) Analyze models of assessment, prevention, intervention, and evaluation;

PB 13. (2.1.3.3) Demonstrated effective oral and written communication in working with individuals, families, groups, organizations, communities, and colleagues;

Competency 4 (EPAS 2.1.4): Engage diversity and difference in practice.

PB 14. (2.1.4.1) Recognize the extent to which a culture's structures and values may oppress, marginalize, alienate, or create or enhance privilege and power;

PB15. (2.1.4.2) Gain sufficient self-awareness to eliminate the influence of personal biases and values in working with diverse groups;

PB 16. (2.1.4.3) Recognize and communicate their understanding of the importance of difference in shaping life experiences;

PB 17. (2.1.4.4) View themselves as learners and engage those with whom they work as informants;

Competency 5 (EPAS 2.1.5): Advance human rights and social and economic justice.

PB 18. (2.1.5.1) Understand the forms and mechanisms of oppression and discrimination;

PB 19. (2.1.5.2) Advocate for human rights and social and economic justice;

PB 20. (2.1.5.3) Engage in practices that advance social and economic justice;

Competency 6 (EPAS 2.1.6): Engage in research-informed practice and practice-informed research.

PB 26.

PB 21. (2.1.6.1) Use practice experiences to inform scientific inquiry;

PB 22. (2.1.6.2) Use research evidence to inform practice;

Competency 7 (EPAS 2.1.7): Apply knowledge of human behavior and the social environment.

PB 23. (2.1.7.1) Utilize conceptual frameworks to guide the process of assessment, intervention, and evaluation;

PB 24. (2.1.7.2) Critique and apply knowledge to understand person and environment;

Competency 8 (EPAS 2.1.8): Engage in policy practice to advance social and economic well-being and to deliver effective social work services.

PB 25. (2.1.8.1) Analyze. Formulate, and advocate for policies that advance social wellbeing;

PB 26. (2.1.8.2) Collaborate with colleagues and clients for effective policy action;

Competency 9 (EPAS 2.1.9): Respond to contexts that shape practice.

PB 27. (2.1.9.1) Continuously discover, appraise, and attend to changing locales, populations, scientific and technological developments, and emerging societal trends to provide relevant services;

PB 28. (2.1.9.2) Provide leadership in promoting sustainable changes in service delivery and practice to improve the quality of social services;

Competency 10 (EPAS 2.1.10): Engage, assess, intervene, and evaluate with individuals, families, groups, organizations and communities.

PB 29. (2.1.10.1) Substantively and effectively prepare for action with individuals, familes, groups, organizations, and communities;

PB 30. (2.1.10.2) Use empathy and other interpersonal skills;

PB 31. (2.1.10.3) Develop a mutually agreed-on focus of work and desired outcomes;

PB 32. (2.1.10.4) Collect, organize and interpret client data;

PB 33. (2.1.10.5) Assess client strengths and limtiations;

PB 34. (2.1.10.6) Develop mutually agreed-on intervention

PB 35. (2.1.10.7) Select appropriate intervention strategies;

PB 36. (2.1.10.8) Initiate actions to achieve organizational goals;

PB 37. (2.1.10.9) Implement prevention interventions that enhance client capacities;

PB 38. (2.1.10.10) Help clients resolve problems;

PB 39. (2.1.10.11) Negotiate, mediate, and advocate for clients;

PB 40. (2.1.10.12) Facilitate transitions and endings;

PB 41. (2.1.10.13) Critically analyze, monitor, and evaluate interventions.

Course Expectations

1. Internship Commitment

Each student intern will complete a minimum of 464 hours in an internship placement setting over one semester. Most students put in 32-hour weeks in four days and take off the day that Senior Seminar is offered. It is mandatory to attend Senior Seminar, but the 32 hour week can be flexibly negotiated between the student and the field instructor in order to best meet the needs of the agency. Regardless of the total hours put in during the semester, the internship must last the duration of the academic semester.

2. Agency Policies and Procedures

Each student intern is required to follow the policies and procedures of the internship agency in which they are placed. If for some reason a student feels he/she cannot comply with an agency policy, the situation must be discussed immediately with the field coordinator/liaison and/or the field instructor.

3. Agency Analysis Paper

The Agency Analysis Paper is an in-depth analysis of the organizational purpose, structure, and roles of the placement agency. This paper is due to the student's field liaison on the fourth Friday of the semester. Failure to receive a passing score or complete this assignment will result in a failed Final grade.

The pape should be typed, double-spaced. Unsatisfactory papers may be returned to the student to be redone. Since the paper is due only four weeks after internship begins, the student will want to start gathering data by reading policy manuals and interviewing agency staff soon after internship begins. This is a 5-8 page paper.

4. Internship Workbook

Students are required to complete an Internship Workbook designed to connect student's practice tasks (specific to their internship placement) to appropriate program practice behaviors/core competencies (see page 23 for a detailed listing).

The workbook is a guide that drives the evaluation process in order to assure a basic level of competency for social work knowledge, values, and skills.

This workbook will also serve as a journal which provides the student an opportunity to reflect on significant internship experiences and connect those experiences to theory, ethics/ethical dilemmas, and evidence-based practice.

The workbook will be presented to the field liaison at the first site visit for review and feedback. The workbook will be turned in with all the final course requirements and must be completed in its entirety to be accepted for a passing grade. Failure to do so will result in a Failed final grade.

5. Policy Advocacy Field Project

The Policy Advocacy Project requires students to independently apply social policy skills in their internship placement setting. This project is due to the student's field liaison on the eighth Friday of the semester. Failure to receive a passing score or complete this assignment will result in a failed Final grade.

Th paper should be typed, double-spaced. Unsatisfactory papers may be returned to the student to be redone. Since the paper requires multiple processes, the student will want to begin formulating their policy analysis soon after internship begins. This is a 5-8 page paper.

6. Agency Site Visits

Two agency site visits by the student's field liaison will occur during the semester. These meetings are arranged by the student and the field liaison, taking into consideration the field instructor's schedule and availability. These meetings allow the field liaison, the field instructor and the student intern an opportunity to review the progress in the internship, discuss mutual expectations of internship, discuss any concerns, and identify future tasks that need to be completed.

The first site visit will occur between the fourth and sixth weeks of internship. Students are expected to be prepared to present and discuss the progress of their internship via the Internship Workbook. This first site visit is a good opportunity for any discussion of concerns and questions that either party may have regarding the internship placement. Additional internship assignments can also be discussed and explored. This meeting usually lasts 45 to 60 minutes. The second site visit will occur between the eleventh and thirteenth weeks of internship. The purpose of this meeting is to check on the progress of internship, to identify what needs to be done before the end of the semester, and to talk about disengagement and termination tasks for the intern as they prepare to leave the internship agency. This meeting usually takes half an hour to complete. This visit may be held as a phone conference call if the situation deems it appropriate.

The field liaison will arrange the site visit meeting times and will coordinate with the field instructor's schedule. It is the responsibility of the student to arrange an alternate time for a site visit should the necessity of cancellation arise.

Internship Meeting

There is one internship meeting with the field coordinator during the semester the students are doing their internship. This meeting is held in conjunction with Senior Seminar. Topics covered usually include social work licensing, Minnesota and ND Merit Exam, preparations for employment, and a review of the assignments for internship. Guest speakers from the Minnesota State Board of Social Work, Clay County Social Services, MSUM Career Services, and North Dakota Department of Human Services usually present more detailed information on these topics at a separate session during Senior Seminar.

7. Evaluation

Students are placed in agencies under the supervision of experienced social services professionals. This allows students to obtain on-going feedback and formal evaluation of their social work knowledge and practice behaviors. The student intern will be formally evaluated twice during the semester, at midterm and the end of the semester. These evaluations use a Likert scale to rate the social work practice behaviors. These evaluation criteria relate directly to the ten program competencies (see page 23 for a detailed listing). This evaluation format will provide students feedback on how they are performing in selected areas, and assist them in identifying those areas that need further development. The Internship Workbook is designed to help guide both the student and the field instructor in their formal evaluation of the 41 practice behaviors (see page 24 for a detailed listing). In addition, each goal has space for any narrative comments the field instructor may have pertaining to the goal.

The field instructor, upon completing the written evaluation, will meet with the student to discuss the evaluation and answer any questions the student may have. Students will also rate themselves using this same form. At the evaluation meeting, the field instructor and the student can then compare their ratings and utilize the discussion for further learning. **The student should remember that the evaluations are not grades. This is an opportunity for feedback and for students to learn a great deal about themselves as potential social workers. Students are strongly encouraged to take maximal advantage of this opportunity. Although the internship evaluations are not grades, the intern's Pass/Fail status will be partially determined by the formal final evaluation results.**

8. Field Instructor Evaluation

The student intern will provide the field instructor with two formal evaluation forms. The midterm evaluation will occur during the eighth week of the semester and the final evaluation will occur the last week of the semester. Students will be evaluated on the ten program competencies through their successful mastery of the 41 practice behaviors of internship. Field Instructors are required to meet and discuss with the student both the mid-term and final evaluations. Upon review and discussion of the evaluation, both parties must sign the Field Instructor Evaluation form. The Internship Workbook is designed to help guide both the field instructor and the student in their formal evaluation of the 41 practice behaviors. The evaluation forms can be found in section VII of the Field Manual. The student is responsible for getting this form to the field instructor on a timely basis. The student is also responsible to ensure that these written evaluations reach the field liaison at midterm and the final week of internship.

9. Student Self Evaluation

Each student will complete two self-evaluations, once at midterm and again at the end of internship. This is the student's assessment of her/his personal learning during the internship in regards to meeting the ten program competencies. The field instructor and student intern will use the same evaluation form in section VII. As stated in the Field Instructor Evaluation section, they will meet and discuss the evaluations with their Field Instructor and both parties must sign the Student Evaluation form. The student will turn all evaluations into the field liaison at the appropriate designated time of the semester.

The field instructor's evaluation, both midterm and final, become part of the student's permanent file.

10. Site Description

Each student will describe the placement agency as an internship site. This is a one to two page typed description that is kept on file in the Social Work Department. There is a form in the back of the manual to guide the student with this required assignment.

This assignment helps the student reflect on the strengths and weaknesses of their placement and provides valuable information to future students who are considering this site for a placement. This assignment is due on the day that final evaluations are due, usually the Friday after the last day of internship. Students are to refer to the outline form provided in Section VII for this description, and are expected to turn in this assignment to the field liaison.

This feedback can be useful for the agency in evaluating its effectiveness as an internship site. However, it is optional for the student to provide the agency with a copy of the site description.

11. Other Evaluations

Each student is asked to fill out several evaluation forms at the end of internship:

Field Liaison evaluation

Field Coordinator/Internship Course evaluation

Field Instructor evaluation

There is also an evaluation for the field instructor to complete on the internship program and the field liaison. These evaluations are in section VII of the Field Manual, and can be turned in with the final evaluations and site description.

Grading

Internship is graded on a pass/fail basis. All of the requirements must be completed on time in a satisfactory manner to obtain a passing grade. Assignments that are unsatisfactory may be returned and the student will be required to redo them. Failure to comply with agency expectations may result in a failing grade. Also, failure to complete the academic expectations may result in a failing grade. Please refer to pages 32 and 33 for information on the Formative Performance Evaluation Deficiency process and the policy and procedures for termination of a student's internship experience.

Approximate Internship Timeline by the Week

Week 1	Week 2-3	Week 4	Week 4-7	Week 8	Week 9-10	Week 11-14	Week 15
Orient to agency		Agency analysis paper due	1st site visit presentation of internship work book.	Miderm evals and policy advocacy project due		2nd site visit	Final evals, internship workbook & site description due

Required Text

Social Work Field Manual, which is available on the MSUM Social Work Department's web page.

Social Work Internship Workbook, available at the MSUM Bookstore

Student Expectations

Field instruction, if it is to be successful, demands the cooperation of a number of different people. Towards this end, the following delineates the major expectations of the student intern in the field education process.

1. Each student is required to follow the policies and procedures of the agency in which he/she is placed. If for some reason, compliance with agency policy is not possible, the student must discuss this immediately with the field coordinator/liaison and/or the field instructor.
2. Students must respect the confidentiality of both the client and the agency.
3. Each student will be expected to understand and facilitate, along with the field coordinator and the field instructor, the successful completion of the field practicum requirements. If the student does not understand the expectations set forth by the course structures, the field coordinator, the field liaison, and/or the field instructor, it is the student's responsibility to clarify the situation.
4. Students are expected to conduct themselves in a professional manner. Professionals take responsibility for understanding their duties and carrying these duties out.
5. Students are expected to be in attendance at the field agency on time, each day indicated by MSUM academic duty days and the field instructor. If the student is ill or unable to attend for another reason, he/

she must notify the field instructor prior to the start of the work day. Likewise, if the student is not able to meet other course expectations, he/she must arrange an exception prior to the expectation deadline with the field coordinator or the field liaison.

6. The student is responsible for completing academic assignments on time and in a satisfactory manner.

B. Internship Flow Chart (by approximate week)

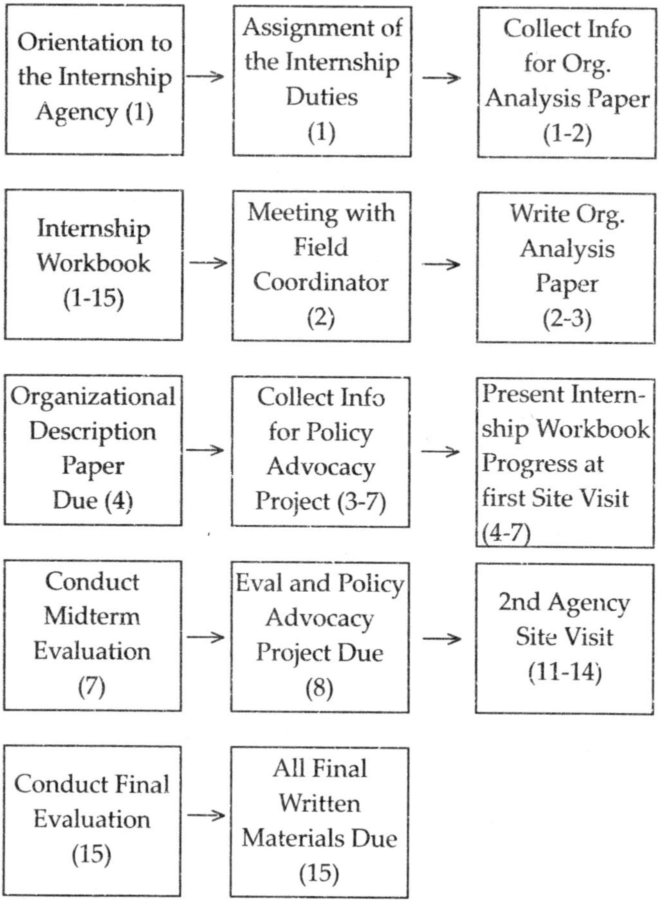

Bibliography

Bogo, M, Vayda, E. (1998). *The practice of field instruction in social work: Theory and process*. New York: Columbia University Press.

Cochrane, S.F., Hanley, M.M. (1999). *Learning through field: A developmental approach*. Boston: Allyn and Bacon.

Dietz, T.J., Westerfelt, A. (1997). *Planning and conducting agency-based research: A workbook for social work students in field placements*. New York: Longman.

Egan, G. (2002). *The Skilled Helper, 7th ed.* United States: Brooks/Cole.

Horejsi, C.R., Garthwait, C.L. (1999). *The social work practicum: A guide and workbook for students*. Boston: Allyn and Bacon.

Kirst-Ashman, K., Hull, G.H. (2002). *Understanding generalist practice*, 3rd *ed*. United States: Brooks/Cole.

Knight, C. (1996) A study of MSW and BSW student's perceptions of their field instructors. *Journal of Social Work Education*, 32(3), 399-414.

Loewenberg, F.M., Dolgoff, R., & Harrington, D. (2000). *Ethical decisions for social work practice*. Illinois: F. E. Peacock Publishers, Inc.

Poorman, P.B. (2003). *Microskills and theoretical foundations for professional helpers*. New York: Allyn and Bacon.

Rea, A. Nicolas-Wolosuk, W. (2003). *Changing agency policy: An incremental approach*. New York: Allyn and Bacon.

Raskin, S. (1994). The Delphi student in field instruction revisited: Expert consensus on issues and research priorities. *Journal of Social Work Education*, 30 (1), 75-89.

Royse, D., Dhooper, S.S., & Rompf, E.L. (1999). *Field instruction: A guide for social work students, 3rd ed.* New York: Longman.

Royse, D. (1995). *Research methods in social work, 2nd ed.* Chicago: Nelson-Hall Publishers. Schneck, D., Grossman, B., Glassman, U. (1991). *Field education in social work: Contemporary issues and trends.*

Kirst-Ashman, K., Hull, G.H. (2002). *Understanding generalist practice,* 3rd *ed.* United States: Brooks/Cole.

Knight, C. (1996) A study of MSW and BSW student's perceptions of their field instructors. *Journal of Social Work Education,* 32(3), 399-414.

Loewenberg, F.M., Dolgoff, R., & Harrington, D. (2000). *Ethical decisions for social work practice.* Illinois: F. E. Peacock Publishers, Inc.

Dubuque: Kendall/Hunt Publishing Company. Sheafor, B.W., Horejsi, C.R. (2003). *Techniques and guidelines for social work practice, 6th ed.* New York: Allyn and Bacon.

Sheafor, B.W., Jenkins, L.E. (1982). *Quality field instruction in social work.* New York & London: Longman.

Strom-Gottfried, K. (1999). *Social work practice.* Thousand Oaks: Pine Forge Press.

Thomlison, B., Rogers, G., Collins, D., & Grinnell, R.M. (1996). *The social work practicum: An access guide*

Westerfelt, A., Dietz, T.J. (1997). *Planning and conducting agency-based research: A workbook for social work students in field placements.* New York: Longman.

Wells, C.C. (1989). *Social work day to day: The experience of generalist social work practice.* New York & London:

Wells, C.C., Masch, M.K. (1991). *Social work ethics day to day: Guidelines for professional practice.* Prospect Heights, Illinois: Waveland Press, Inc.

Internship Assignments Timeframe

Meeting with Field Coordinator (and Liaisons)

Occurs on the 2nd Friday of the semester during Senior Seminar.

Fourth Friday of the semester

Agency Analysis Paper due to Field Liaison

First Site Visit with Field Liaison

Occurs during the 4th – 6th weeks of the semester (possibly the 7th, as well)

Presentation of Internship Workbook progress

Midterm

Due the 8th Friday of the semester to Field Liaison

- Policy Advocacy Project Due
- Field Instructor's Evaluation (signed by BOTH parties)
- Student's Self Evaluation (signed by BOTH parties)

Second Site Visit with Field Liaison

Occurs during the 11th – 13th weeks of internship (possibly the 14th, as well)

*note: this visit may be held as a conference call with long distance internshipsv unless an on-site visit is deemed necessary by the Field Liaison

Final

Due date is the first exam day of finals week

- Internship Workbook
- Field Instructor's Evaluation (signed by BOTH parties)
- Student's Self Evaluation (signed by BOTH parties)
- Site Description
- Student's Evaluation of Field Instructor

- Student's Evaluation of Field Program/Field Coordinator
- Student's Evaluation of Field Liaison
- Field Instructor's Evaluation of the Field Program

C. Internship Goals

Internship is designed to allow significant flexibility in the type of experiences and social work content the student can obtain. Students will be placed in a variety of different internship sites with various opportunities for learning. Each social work student, however, will have the opportunity for professional education in each of the following ten competency areas:

1. (EPAS 2.1.1). Identify as a professional social worker and conduct oneself accordingly;
2. (EPAS 2.1.2) Apply social work ethical principles to guide professional practice;
3. (EPAS 2.1.3) Apply critical thinking to inform and communicate professional judgments;
4. (EPAS 2.1.4) Engage diversity and difference in practice;
5. (EPAS 2.1.5) Advance human rights and social and economic justice;
6. (EPAS 2.1.6) Engage in research-informed practice and practice-informed research;
7. (EPAS 2.1.7) Apply knowledge of human behavior and the social environment;
8. (EPAS 2.1.8) Engage in policy practice to advance social and economic well-being and to deliver

effective social work services;

9. (EPAS 2.1.9) Respond to contexts that shape practice;

The social work internship provides a structure for students to obtain significant feedback regarding their practice skills. Students unaccustomed to getting feedback regarding their behavior may initially feel threatened by this process. However, students intent on learning as much as they can from internship will seek out opportunities to obtain this feedback.

Feedback is a critical element in the learning process. In addition to feedback, the competent social worker must have regular supervision from an experienced supervisor. Social work supervision is important for two reasons. First, social workers, no matter how well trained, cannot have expertise in every situation they encounter. An experienced supervisor can be an invaluable source of information. Secondly, when social workers are in the midst of working with intense situations, they can lose perspective. A social work supervisor can assist in restoring the case perspective.

This feedback and supervision will be provided through three primary structures:

1. Students will obtain regular supervision of their work in the internship from the field instructor.
2. Two formal written evaluations of the student's work will be completed by the field instructor and the student.

3. The field coordinator and/or field liaison will provide written feedback to the student on all written materials required for internship completion.

In addition, Child Welfare grant recipients will receive feedback from the Child Welfare Director.

Notes

Chapter 5

Field Instruction/Field Liasion/Field Coordinator

A. Placement Agency Expectations

1. The agency must provide a sanctioned social service or criminal justice program.
2. The agency must provide qualified personnel to be assigned as "Field Instructor" for the student intern.
3. The agency is willing to follow the procedures as outlined in the field manual.

4. The agency will provide students with a description of the agency's expectations and anticipated duties for a bachelors level social work intern.
5. The agency understands that internship is an academic course. As such, the student's primary focus is professional education and training. Although it can be expected that students will assume numerous responsibilities which benefit the agency, they are not employees who will fill the needs of an understaffed agency.
6. A placement contract is required of each agency in order to place student interns. This contract sets out the parameters for the cooperative arrangement between the School of Social Work, the field agency and the student intern.
7. The agency agrees to follow the policy and procedures related to termination of a student from the field placement and the policies related to sexual harassment. The agency further agrees to follow the structures outlined in this field manual.

B. Field Instructor Expectations

1. The School of Social Work requires that field instructors have a college degree, preferably a Bachelor's or Master's degree in Social Work. If the field instructor does not possess a social work degree, he/she agrees to provide a field experience which is consistent with social work values and ethics. The NASW Code of Ethics will be provided to non-SW field instructors.
2. The field instructor is responsible for orienting the student to the agency and assigning the student responsibilities for internship in which the student will be able to successfully demonstrate achievement of the required Core Competencies/Practice Behaviors. Each

field instructor will fill out the Internship Activities/ Expectations form to facilitate student role clarity.

3. The agency field instructor must commit to assisting the student in integrating the social work knowledge, values and skills obtained in the classroom in an agency setting through supervision and planning with the student. A minimum of one hour of weekly individual supervision is expected.
4. Field instructors are invited to participate in seminars and workshops designed by the School of Social Work which facilitate an understanding of the social work curriculum and requirements of the internship. New field instructors are required to attend the first orientation seminar before a student is placed in the agency.
5. Field instructors are expected to formally evaluate students twice during the semester, at midterm and at the end of the semester. An explanation of the evaluation process can be found on page 78. The midterm and final evaluation form can be found in Section VII. The field instructor will be expected to meet with the student to discuss each evaluation.
6. At the end of the semester, field instructors are asked to evaluate the field coordinator's performance in facilitating the field practicum and the field liaisons performance (section VIII).
7. Field instructors are expected to follow the structures outlined in this manual for internship and field experience.

C. The Social Work Field Learning Model

Field instruction is primarily learning by doing which is much different from other university courses the students have experienced which has been learning through lecture and reading. Since a different method of learning is utilized in field instruction, a learning model that is much different from the classroom model is utilized. Because the student is developing social work knowledge, values and skills in the agency setting, field instruction is directed by social work ethics, eco-systemic theory and the generalist practice model of problem-solving. This section describes these elements of the social work field learning model.

1. Social Work Ethics

The NASW Code of Ethics provides guidelines for the ethical practice of social work. Students have been introduced to this code in their social work classes, and will be studying it in more depth in senior seminar class during the course of internship. The relevance of the code to professional practice oftentimes does not become apparent until the student actually experiences ethical dilemmas in practice. Internship and field experience provide the opportunity for students to wrestle with the demands of competing interests, priorities and commitments.

2. Eco-systemic Theory

The eco-systemic theory refers to the theoretical foundations of social work practice. Social workers are not only concerned with the individual client or client system, but are concerned how other systems (i.e. biological, psychological, and/or social) impact or influence the functioning of the identified client. Although many social work programs are designed to intervene primarily in one system, the effective social worker is constantly assessing and reassessing the influences of other systems on the client's functioning. This attention to the whole client system is critical to the development of appropriate case plans that address client needs and the identification of the need for referral to other service providers.

3. The Social Work Generalist Practice Model

This model is the problem-solving model taught in the MSUM social work program. It is used in the social work methods courses as a common orienting point for working with social work client systems (i.e. individuals, families, groups, communities and organizations). Each social work agency has its own format for insuring that these elements are covered when working with clients. These elements include: Assessment, Goal-setting, Planning, Implementation, and Evaluation.

Therefore the social work field learning model has three major orienting components: the NASW Code of Ethics, the eco-systemic theory, and the generalist practice model of problem solving. Both internship and the field experience courses are structured with these three conceptual frameworks in mind.

The placement agency and field instructor provide a context capable of administering these structures which results in the professional education of social work students.

In addition to these three components, there is a fourth concept that is a part of the learning model, and that is the concept of feedback. Field instruction is designed to give students significant feedback regarding their performance in a social work role. To insure sufficient feedback which will help the student experience "integrative learning", a collaborative partnership between the student, the placement agency and the MSUM Social Work Department is formed.

Each person in this partnership has responsibilities regarding feedback:

1. The student is responsible for identifying and communicating their learning objectives, and providing

feedback regarding the progress towards these objectives.

2. The social work department is responsible for identifying the goals of professional social work education and providing feedback regarding the progress towards these goals.

3. The placement agency is responsible for identifying and communicating the professional competencies necessary for a social worker in the agency, and providing feedback regarding progress towards these competencies.

The placement agency designates a field instructor (or field supervisor) who takes primary responsibility for the agency's part in this learning process. The MSUM Social Work Department designates a field liaison who takes primary responsibility for the department's commitment to student learning. The feedback necessary for learning is transmitted via the relationships formed by these three parties.

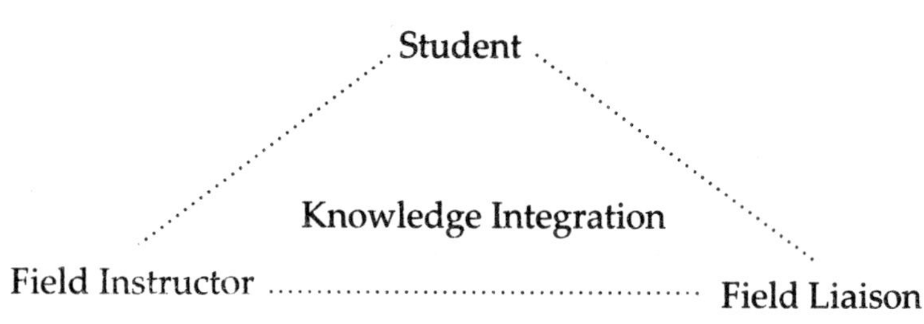

To be successful, this process demands the active participation of all three parties. If everyone works together, actively giving and receiving feedback, the end result is the integration of knowledge and the development of competencies necessary for the practice of professional social work.

D. Tips on Supervision

Take time to orient your student intern to the agency, introducing her/him to staff.

Be sure that your student intern has his/her own nametag, identifying him/her as a social work intern.

Set up regular times for conferences with your student intern, at least weekly for one on one meeting. If possible, avoid telephone interruptions.

Let your student intern know that you expect some thinking on his/her part before s/he comes to these conferences, and that your role is a helping one, not a directing one.

Respect boundaries: a teacher/learner relationship must be maintained so that learning will remain the primary focus of the internship experience.

One of the primary goals of supervision is to formulate a sound educational plan as quickly as possible. The student intern will formulate a Learning Plan in the first several weeks of internship based on the goals of internship. Meet with your student intern and discuss this learning plan.

Be careful not to supervise in terms of your own needs, but in terms of the intern's needs. This means being aware of the student's learning plan and helping him/her meet their objectives.

The student intern's personal problems may need to be looked at, but counseling or therapy is inappropriate. Consult with the field liaison if student's personal problems are interfering with the internship experience.

Let the student intern know that you are available to them in an emergency.

Review the student intern's caseload on a regular basis. Students should keep notes re: their caseload, their impressions, afterthoughts about things they might have handled differently, things they still need to know, etc.

Move through the supervisory process toward independent functioning for the intern.

It is always a good idea to document. Write up notes of conferences with your student intern. Keep a record of his/her performance.

Help the student intern to learn to think for him/herself.

Remember: **Respect boundaries - a teacher/learner relationship must be maintained so that learning will remain the primary focus.**

E. Evaluation Process

The student intern will be formally evaluated twice during the semester, at midterm and the end of the semester. Evaluation of the internship experience reflects the students' ability to achieve successful integration and application of the ten program competencies (see page 34 for a detailed listing) in an actual practice setting. Each program competency will ultimately be evaluated by rating the related practice behaviors associated with it (see page 35 for a detailed listing of the practice behaviors). These evaluations use a Likert scale to rate each specific social work practice behaviors.

This evaluation format will provide students feedback on how they are performing in selected areas, and assist them in identifying those areas that need further development. The Internship Workbook is designed to help guide both the field instructor and the student in their formal evaluation of the 41 practice behaviors. In addition, each goal has space for any narrative comments the field instructor may have pertaining to the goal.

The field instructor, upon completing the written evaluation, will meet with the student to discuss the evaluation and answer any question the student may have. Students will also rate themselves using this same form. At the evaluation meeting, the field instructor and the student can then compare their ratings and utilize the discussion for further learning. The student should remember that the evaluations are not grades.

This is an opportunity for feedback and for students to learn a great deal about themselves as potential social workers. Students are strongly encouraged to take maximal advantage of this opportunity. Although the internship evaluations are not grades, the interns' Pass/Fail status will be partially determined by the formal final evaluation results.

Field Instructor Evaluation

The student intern will provide the field instructor with two formal evaluation forms. The midterm evaluation will occur during the eighth week of the semester and the final evaluation will occur the last week of the semester. Students will be evaluated on the ten program competencies through their successful mastery of the 41 practice behaviors of internship.

Field Instructors are required to meet and discuss with the student both the mid-term and final evaluations. Upon review and discussion of the evaluation, both parties must sign the Field Instructor Evaluation form. The Internship Workbook is designed to help guide both the field instructor and the student in their formal evaluation of the 41 practice behaviors. The evaluation forms can be found in section

VII of the Field Manual. The student is responsible for getting this form to the field instructor on a timely basis. The student is also responsible to ensure that these written evaluations reach the field liaison at midterm and the final week of internship.

Student Self Evaluation

Each student will complete two self-evaluations, once at midterm and again at the end of internship. This is the student's assessment of her/his personal learning during the internship in regards to meeting the ten program competencies. The field instructor and student intern will use the same evaluation form in section VII. As stated in the Field Instructor Evaluation section, they will meet and discuss the evaluations with their Field Instructor and both parties must sign the Student Evaluation form. The student will turn all evaluations into the field liaison at the appropriate designated time of the semester. (cont.)

The field instructor's evaluation, both midterm and final, become part of the student's permanent file.

F. Field Liaison Expectations

The field liaison is the person who follows student interns in their field placement. This person is a member of the MSUM Social Work department faculty. The expectations of the field liaison are:

1. Responsible for two site visits to the placement agency during the semester to review the progress of internship or field experience with the student and the field instructor.
2. Responsible for providing written feedback to students on all written assignments.
3. Responsible for providing the field coordinator the assigned course grade (pass /fail) for the students.

4. Available to field students and field instructors to provide consultation regarding field placement and to facilitate the resolution of problems that may arise. The field liaison can consult with and include the field coordinator in these situations.
5. Responsible for keeping files on all students in field liaison's intern assignment load and keeping student's internship/field experience application, contract, learning plan, and field instructor's evaluations in these files. These files will be provided to the field liaison by the field coordinator prior to internship/field experience. These files will be returned to the field coordinator at the end of the semester.

G. Field Coordinator Expectations

The field coordinator assumes responsibility for the overall direction and coordination of internship and field experience. This person is a faculty member of the MSUM Social Work Department and is available to students, field instructors, and field liaisons, to assist them in the internship and/or field experience placements. The field coordinator also follows a number of student interns in their placements, serving as their field liaison.

The expectations for the field coordinator include:

1. Responsible for the overall direction and coordination of the internship and field experience.
2. Responsible for the on-going evaluation of field practicum experiences and maintaining the Field Manual.
3. Available to field students and field instructors to provide consultation regarding field placement and to facilitate the resolution of problems that may arise.
4. Responsible for arranging and facilitating the field

instructor seminars during the semester.

5. Responsible for arranging and facilitating the meeting of student interns and the field coordinator during the semester.
6. Responsible for arranging and facilitating the student internship preparation meetings for students planning their internship.
7. Responsible for assigning the course grade (Pass / Fail).
8. Responsible for removal of a student from a placement, should that become necessary.
9. When acting as field liaison, responsible for two site visits during the semester to the placement agency to review the progress of internship with the student and field instructor.

Chapter 6

Forms

A. Second Human Service Experience
B. Internship/Field Experience Application
C. Letter of Intent for Prospective Placements
D. Internship/Field Experience Finalization Information
E. Internship/Field Experience Contract with Placement Agencies
F. Internship Activities / Expectations
G. Internship Midterm and Final Evaluation
H. Site Description of the Internship Agency
I. Student's Evaluation of Field Instructor
J. Student's Evaluation of Field Program / Field Coordinator
K. Student's Evaluation of the Field Liaison
L. Field Instructor's Evaluation of the Field Program

SECOND HUMAN SERVICE EXPERIENCE

Student Name: ______________________

Agency Name: ______________________

Dates of Experience: ________ to __________

Total hours of experience: ______________________

Brief description of activities and responsibilities in the completion of this experience:

How would you evaluate this student's performance of assigned duties?

Did student successfully complete the requirements of this experience? Yes ___ No ___

If you marked no, please explain.

____________________ ______

(Supervisor's Signature) Date

SE 469: INTERNSHIP
SCHOOL OF SOCIAL WORK
MINNESOTA STATE UNIVERSITY MOORHEAD

Date Submitted:

____

Semester and year of placement: __________________

SW 469 Internship 12 credits

____

(first name) (middle initial) (last)

Current Address: ____________________________

____

Phone: ____________________________

MSUM E-mail address:* ________________________

*Please note that all official MSUM business is conducted via Dragon Mail.

Present class rank (yr.) ________________________

Anticipated graduation date ______________________

MSUM GPA __________Advisor's Name __________

Number of Human Service Hours Completed________

What areas of social work are of special interest to you? (Explain)

____

____

____

In what geographic area are you interested in interning?

____

I understand that I will be required to participate in three internship planning meetings and complete all preparatory assignments on time.

I understand that MSUM does not provide medical insurance unless I have elected to purchase it.

I understand that MSUM provides a limited amount of liability insurance.

I understand that I am required to do my internship/field placement within a radius of 250 miles from the Fargo-Moorhead area.

I understand that it is my responsibility to get enrolled in another University's Senior Seminar course from an accredited Social Work program if I do not take MSUM's course.

I understand that failure to honor this agreement may result in the postponement of my internship experience.

______________________ ______

Signature of Applicant Date

Do not Write Below this Line

Approved ______

Not Approved ______

Comments:

___________________________ ______

Signature of Field Coordinator Date

MINNESOTA STATE UNIVERSITY

Moorhead

Date:________

To: __________
____
____

Re: ____________________
MSUM Social Work Student
Semester of Internship_____
From_________to________

Minnesota State University Moorhead social work students are currently making initial inquire regarding potential internship placements. Internship is a required course in the School of Social Work. It involves one full semester (15 weeks) of full time (32 hours a week) supervised experience in a human service agency. The student receives 12 credits for the internship.

The above named student is requesting the opportunity to be interviewed by you and learn more about your agency's programs and services, and to be considered for an internship at your agency. This interview will help provide information to both the student and the agency regarding the potential "fit" of their respective interests and needs. Attached to this letter is the student's resume.

This initial inquiry begins the process for internship. Once a student completes his/her interviews and decides on an agency, he/she meets with me and completes some finalization forms. I then contact the chosen agency to finalize the internship. It will be your responsibility to contact the student following the interview with your decision.

Thank you very much for your time and interest in discussing your agency and possible internship placements with our students. If you have any questions, please contact me at (218) 477-4002 or clarkt@mnstate.edu .

Sincerely,

Tracy Clark

Field Coordinator/Assistant Professor

Internship/Field Experience Finalization Information

Student Information

Name

____

Address

____

City / State / Zip

____

Phone Number

____

Email Address

____

I wish to finalize my placement for____ semester, 20______

Placement Agency Information

Field Instructors Name(s)

____

Academic Degree of Field Instructor

____

Agency Name

____

Program Name (if any)

____

Address

____

City / State / Zip

____

Phone Number

____

Background Check (MN Agency)________Date Completed

For Department Use Only

____ Field Manual ____ Contract Mailed

____ Activities/Expectations Form ___ Contract Returned

____ Parking Permit

Internship or Field Experience Contract with Placement Agencies

1. Social Work Department
   Minnesota State University Moorhead
   Moorhead, MN 56563
   (218) 477-2632 Fax: (218) 477-2987

2. Agency Name ______________________
   Address ______________________

   ____

Phone ______________________

3. Student Name ______________________

Address ______________________

____

Phone ______________________

This contract is established between the above parties and applies to the requirements of :

SW 469 – Field Internship

for ____________ semester, 20____________

The internship/field experience begins on ____________ and ends on ____________.

It is mutually agreed that the above named agency will provide the following services and supervision:

1. Orientation to the agency will be provided and specific student duties defined.
2. Field instructor(s) within the agency will be:

____

____

3. Field Instructors will attend, whenever possible, field seminars presented by MSUM Department of Social Work designed to enhance field instruction. New Field Instructors will attend the Field Instructor Orientation meeting prior to internship placement.
4. Written evaluations will be completed and either returned directly to the social work department by the above named field instructor(s) or through the student, at midterm and the end of the semester.
5. Because the primary focus is professional education and training, the field instructor is responsible for orienting the student to the agency and assigning the student responsibilities for internship in which the student will be able to successfully demonstrate achievement of the required Core Competencies/Practice Behaviors.
6. The agency field instructor must commit to assisting the student in integrating the social work knowledge, values and skills obtained in the classroom in an agency setting through supervision and planning with the student. A minimum of one hour of weekly individual supervision
7. Each agency reserves the right to terminate an internship placement as deemed appropriate by their individual agency needs and/or policies.
8. Any major changes in assignment or termination of internship by the agency need to include consultation with the student's field liaison and field coordinator.

It is agreed that the student will:

Each student intern will complete a minimum of 464 hours in an internship placement settingover one semester. Most students put in 32-hour weeks in four days and take off the day that Senior Seminar is offered. It is mandatory to attend Senior Seminar, but the 32 hour week can be flexibly negotiated between the student and the field instructor in order to best meet the needs of the agency. Regardless of the total hours put in during the semester, the internship must last the duration of the academic semester.

Each student will:

1. Report to the agency at the dates and times specified by the field instructor.
2. Perform the social work intern duties assigned by the field instructor.
3. Follow placement agency policies and procedures.
4. Take responsibility for understanding the expectations set forth by the course structures, the field coordinator and liaison, and / or field instructor.
5. Conduct him/herself in a professional manner.
6. Take responsibility for completing internship/field experience assignments on time and in a manner.
7. Be involved in the evaluation process with the field instructor.
8. Write an evaluation of the student's experience in the agency to be submitted to the field coordinator at the end of the semester.

It is also agreed that Minnesota State University Moorhead Department of Social Work will provide the following:

1. Advise students as to the requirements involved in the internship or field experience courses.
2. Advise students regarding the types of agencies available for placement, various client groups served and the responsibilities of the students in placement.
3. Contact the agency to arrange and / or assist in planning the internship or field experience.

4. Provide internship agencies / field instructors with updated Field Manuals.
5. Provide faculty field liaisons who will maintain periodic contacts with the field instructor and the student to discuss the progress and to offer support to both the student and field instructor.
6. Give the student feedback regarding departmental supervision and maintain appropriate records for registration and grading.
7. Initiate and receive background checks as designated by MSUM policies (section Q in this handbook) and/or agency policies.

Please check if your agency is licensed by the following:

_____ MN Department of Human Services

_____ MN Department of Health

The following signatures verify agreement to the conditions stated on pages one and two.

Student________________________

Date________________

____

Agency Director______________

Date________________

____

Agency Field Instructor_________

Date________________

____

MSUM Field Coordinator_________

Date________________

Internship Activities / Expectations

Agency / Program Name

____

Field Instructor Name (s)

____

Student Intern

____

This is not a student job description or a contract with the student, but is rather an attempt to give some direction to the student intern regarding your vision of the important elements of a social work internship at your agency/program.

What activities might the student expect to experience while at this internship site? (i.e. client assessment, intervention activities, group work, etc.)

____

____

What meetings might the student expect to attend and/or participate in at this site?

____

____

____

____

____

____

What trainings in-services, and supervision might the student experience at this site?

____

____

____

What is the dress code at your agency?

____

____

____

If you are not available, to whom should the social work intern turn to for help and guidance?

____

____

____

What are your expectations of the social work intern?

____

____

____

____

____

Other comments:

____

____

____

____

____

____

____

Please include a copy of this document with the contract nd return both items to the field coordinator at MSUM. On the first day of internship, please give a copy of this document to your social work intern.

School of Social Work
Minnesota State University Moorhead
SW 469 Internship Evaluation

Student Name: ________________Date: _______________

Field Instructor Name: ______________________________

Agency: ____

Please check one in each category:

a. Field Instructor Evaluation _____ or Student Self Evaluation _____

b. Midterm Evaluation _____ or Final Evaluation _____

Rating of this internship experience reflects the students' ability to achieve successful integration and application of the ten program competencies in an actual practice setting. Each program competency will ultimately be evaluated by rating the resulting practice behaviors associated with it.

Rating Scale:

5 = Section work shows *exemplary* achievement of baccalaureate-level practice skills and competencies

4 = Section work shows *above average* achievement of baccalaureate-level practice skills and competencies

3 = Section work shows *average* achievement of baccalaureate-level practice skills and competencies

2 = Section work shows *below average* achievement of baccalaureate-level practice skills and competencies

1 = Section work shows no achievement of baccalaureate-level practice skills and competencies

1. (2.1.1). Identify as a professional social worker and conduct oneself accordingly;

PB 1. Advocate for client access to the services of

(2.1.1.1) social work;__________

PB 2. Practice personal reflection and self-correction

(2.1.1.2) Continual professional development; _______

PB 3. Attend to professional roles and

(2.1.1.3) boundaries;__________

PB 4 Demonstrate professional demeanor in:

(2.1.1.4) a. Behavior __________

b. Appearance _______

c. Communication_____

PB.5. Engage in career-long learning;____________

(2.1.1.5)

PB 6. Use supervision and consultation;__________

(2.1.1.6)

Comments:

____

____

2. (2.1.2) Apply social work ethical principles to guide professional practice;

PB 7. Recognize and personal values in a way that allows

(2.1.2.1) professional values to guide practice;________

PB 8. Make ethical decisions by applying standards of

(2.1.2.2) NASW Code of Ethics; __________________

PB 9. Tolerate ambiguity in resolving ethical conflicts;

(2.1.2.3)

PB 10. Apply strategies of ethical reasoning to

(2.1.2.4) arrive at principled decisions; _______________

Comments:

____

____

3. (2.1.3.) Apply critical thinking to inform and communicate professional judgments;

PB 11. Distinguish, appraise, and integrate multiple sources
(2.1.3.1) knowledge, including researchbased
knowledge, and practice wisdom; ____________

PB 12. Analyze models of assessment, prevention,
(2.1.3.2) intervention, and evaluation; ____________

PB 13. Demonstrated effective oral communication in
(2.1.3.3) working with:

a. Individuals ____________

b. Families ____________

c. Groups ____________

d. Organizations ____________

e. Commiunities ____________

f. Colleagues ____________

Demonstrated effective written communication in working with:

g. Individuals ____________

h. Families ____________

i. Groups ____________

j. Organizations ____________

k. Communities ____________

l. Colleagues ____________

Comments:

____

____

____

4. (2.1.4) Engage diversity and difference in practice;

PB 14. Recognize the extent to which a culture's structures
(2.1.4.1) values may oppress_____ marginalize, alienate,
or create enhance privilege and power; ____________
PB 15. Gain sufficient self-awareness to eliminate the
(2.1.4.2) influence of personal biases and values in
working with diverse groups; ____________________
PB 16. Recognize and communicate their understanding
(2.1.4.3) the importance of difference in shaping life
experiences; _________
PB 17. View themselves as learners and engage those with
(2.1.4.4) whom they work as informants; ___________

Comments:

____

____

5. (2.1.5) Advance human rights and social and economic justice;

PB 18. Understand the forms and mechanisms of
(2.1.5.1) oppression and discrimination; _____________
PB 19. Advocate for human rights and social and
(2.1.5.2) economic justice; _____________________
PB 20. Engage in practices that advance social and
(2.1.5.3) economic justice; _____________________

Comments:

____

____

6. (2.1.6) Engage in research-informed practice and practice-informed research;

PB 21. Use practice experiences to inform
(2.1.6.1) scientific inquiry; _____________________
PB 22. Use research evidence to inform

(2.1.6.2) practice; ______________________

Comments:

____

____

____

7. (2.1.7) Apply knowledge of human behavior and the social environment;

PB 23. Utilize conceptual frameworks to guide the process
(2.1.7.1) of assessment, intervention, and evaluation; _____
PB 24. Critique and apply knowledge to understand
(2.1.7.2) person and environment; ______________

Comments:

____

____

____

8. (2.1.8.) Engage in policy practice to advance social and economic well-being and to deliver effective social work services;

PB 25. Analyze. Formulate, and advocate for policies
(2.1.8.1) that advance social well-being; ______________
PB 26. Collaborate with colleagues and clients
(2.1.8.2) for effective policy action;______________

Comments:

____

____

____

9. (2.1.9) Respond to contexts that shape practice;

PB 27. Continuously discover, appraise, and attend to
(2.1.9.1) changing locales, populations, scientific and
technological developments, and emerging

societal trends to provide relevant services; __________
PB 28. Provide leadership in promoting sustainable changes (2.1.9.2) in service delivery and practice to improve the quality of social services;_______________

Comments:

____

____

____

10. (2.1.10)Engage, assess, intervene, and evaluate with individuals, families, groups, organizations and communities;

PB 29. Substantively and effectively prepare for action with: (2.1.10.1)

a. Individuals __________________

b. Families __________________

c. Groups __________________

d. Organizations __________________

e. Communities __________________

PB 30. Use empathy and other interpersonal skills; _____ (2.1.10.2)
PB 31. Develop a mutually agreed-on focus of (2.1.10.3) work and desired outcomes; _______________
PB 32. Collect, organize and interpret client data; ________
PB 33. Assess client strengths and limtiations; __________ (2.1.10.5)
PB 34. Develop mutually agreed-on intervention (2.1.10.6) goals and objectives; _________________
PB 35. Select appropriate intervention strategies;_________ (2.1.10.7)
PB 36. Initiate actions to achieve (2.1.10.8) organizational goals; _____________________

PB 37. Implement prevention interventions (2.1.10.9) that enhance client capacities; ____________

PB 38. Help clients resolve problems; ______________ (2.1.10.10)

PB 39. Negotiate, mediate, and advocate for clients; ______ (2.1.10.11)

PB 40. Facilitate transitions and endings; ____________ (2.1.10.12)

PB 41. Critically analyze, monitor, and (2.1.10.13) evaluate interventions. _________________

Comments:

____

____

____

Any additional comments regarding student performance

____

____

____

Signatures:

______________________________ ______

Field Instructor or Student Date

I have reviewed this evaluation:

______________________________ ______

Student or Field Instructor Date

Site Description of the Internship Agency

Agency:

____

City and State:

____

Student (optional)

____

Date

____

1. What is the mission of the agency?

2. Briefly describe the activities in which you were involved during your experience. Identify the client groups served and your role in that service provision.

3. Consider the supervision you received during your placement and what you learned from it.

4. Recommendations which might be made to improve this setting. Would you recommend this setting for future interns?

Student's Evaluation of Field Instructor

Student's Name ___________________________

Field Instructor's Name ___________________________

Date ___________________________

1. Evaluate the quality of supervision you received during your internship. (i.e. Was supervision regular enough? Was there sufficient time to get answers to questions? Did you get enough direction, feedback, etc.?)

2. What level of support did you receive from your field instructor in your role as an intern? (i.e. Did your field instructor support your case decisions? Did your field instructor take steps to protect you in situations where your inexperience placed you at risk? Etc.)

3. How much and in what ways did your field instructor challenge you to learn?

4. Other comments?

Student's Evaluation of Field Program/Field Coordinator

Name of Field Coordinator ______________________
Semester and year of placement______________________
SW 469-Internship ______________________

1. How would you evaluate the field coordinator's preparation meetings before you started internship, and the follow-up meeting during your internship? (Were they helpful? Well presented? Clear information? Etc.)

2. Were the course expectations clear? If not, were you able to obtain clarification from the field coordinator?

3. Were the written assignments useful to your learning? How so or why not?

4. Other comments about the course and/or the field coordinator:

Student's Evaluation of Field Liaison

Name of Field Liaison ______________________

Semester and year of placement ______________________

1. On the basis of your experiences as an intern, how

would you evaluate the field liaison's contacts with you? (Were the on-site visits helpful? Was the field liaison supportive of you? Available to you when needed? Etc.)

2. What is your evaluation of the field liaison's relationship with your field instructor?

3. What is your view of the field liaison as a professional role model?

4. Other comments about your field liaison:

Field Instructor's Evaluation of the Field Program

Name ____

Agency ______________________________________

Student Intern Name ___________________________

Date ____

On the basis of your experiences with (Field Liaison person) What is your evaluation of his/her performance in the following areas:

1. Ability to work with and assist you in accomplishing

the educational objectives of internship:

2. Ability to work with the student intern:

3. Ability to establish a good working relationship between the agency and the university which enhanced the learning and advanced the goals of the student intern.

4. Other comments regarding the field liaison person:

On the basis of your experience with (Field Coordinator) ____________ what is your evaluation of his/her performance in the following areas?

1. Ability to give clear information to you regarding the expectations of a field instructor. (initial contact, the contract, the field manual, the orientation field instructors meeting, etc.)

2. Ability to be available in assisting you, your field liaison, and/ or the student intern regarding concerns about the internship.

3. Other comments:

Thank you for your valuable input. Your comments are important to the success of our internship program. Thank you also for serving as field instructor.

Index